Pet Breeding for Profits: The Entrepreneur's Guide to Dog Sales

AF409226

Copyright Page

TITLE: Pet Breeding for Profits: The Entrepreneur's Guide to Dog Sales

1ST Edition

Copyright @ 2023

Roberto M. Rodriguez. All rights reserved.

ISBN: 9798223935858

Table of Contents

Pet Breeding for Profits: The Entrepreneur's Guide to Dog Sales

By Roberto Miguel Rodriguez

Chapter 1: Introduction to Designer Dog Breeding

The History and Evolution of Crossbreeding Canines

In the fascinating world of dog breeding, the practice of crossbreeding canines has a rich and storied history. This subchapter delves into the intriguing past and the remarkable evolution of this art, shedding light on the various aspects that have shaped the breeds we know and love today.

Crossbreeding, also known as hybrid breeding, involves mating two different purebred dogs to create a new breed with desired traits from both parents. This practice dates back centuries, with the precise origins lost to time. However, evidence suggests that crossbreeding was a common practice in ancient civilizations such as the Egyptians, Greeks, and Romans.

Throughout history, crossbreeding has served various purposes. In the early days, it was primarily driven by necessity. For instance, hunters needed dogs with specific skills, such as scent tracking or retrieving. By mixing different breeds, they could create dogs that excelled in these specialized tasks. This led to the development of notable crossbreeds like the Labrador Retriever and the Golden Retriever.

Over time, crossbreeding evolved beyond utilitarian purposes and into the realm of aesthetics and companionship. The emergence of designer dogs, such as the Labradoodle and the Cockapoo, marked a turning point in the crossbreeding landscape. These breeds were intentionally created to combine the best traits of their parent breeds, such as hypoallergenic coats or friendly temperaments.

The rise of designer dog breeding sparked a surge in popularity among dog owners seeking unique and personalized companions. Today, there is a plethora of crossbreeds to choose from, each with its own distinctive characteristics and appeal.

However, it is crucial to approach crossbreeding responsibly and ethically. Breeders should prioritize the health and well-being of the dogs, ensuring proper genetic testing and screening to minimize the risk of inherited diseases. Additionally, breeders should be knowledgeable about the breed standards and work towards maintaining consistent traits in their crossbred dogs.

For those involved in small breed dog breeding, large breed dog breeding, or rare breed dog breeding, crossbreeding can present exciting opportunities to enhance and diversify their programs. Show dog breeders can explore the potential of crossbreeds to bring fresh perspectives to the ring. Working and service dog breeders can harness the benefits of mixing breeds to create specialized working partners with specific skill sets.

In conclusion, the history and evolution of crossbreeding canines have shaped the dog breeding world we know today. From its humble beginnings rooted in necessity to the current era of designer dog breeding, crossbreeding has provided dog owners with a vast array of choices and unique companions. However, responsible breeding practices and ethical considerations should always guide the creation of these crossbreeds, ensuring the health and happiness of the dogs involved.

The Appeal and Popularity of Designer Dogs

In recent years, designer dogs have taken the canine world by storm, capturing the hearts of dog owners from all walks of life. These unique crossbreeds have become increasingly popular among various niches, including small breed dog breeding, large breed dog breeding, purebred dog breeding, and even service dog breeding. Their charm and allure stem from their distinctive combination of traits, making them the perfect companion for individuals with specific needs or preferences.

One of the main reasons for the appeal of designer dogs is their ability to inherit the best qualities from both parent breeds. For example, a cross between a poodle and a golden retriever, often referred to as a Goldendoodle, can possess the intelligence and trainability of a poodle along with the friendly and affectionate nature of a golden retriever. This unique blend allows dog owners to enjoy the best of both worlds, creating a one-of-a-kind companion.

Designer dogs also offer a wider range of options for individuals seeking specific characteristics in their canine companions. Whether it's a hypoallergenic coat, a smaller size suitable for apartment living, or a particular temperament for therapy work, there is likely a designer dog breed that can meet those requirements. This versatility has made designer dogs popular among breeders and dog owners alike.

Furthermore, the rising popularity of designer dogs has also contributed to the preservation of rare and endangered dog breeds. By carefully selecting parent breeds, breeders can create crossbreeds that carry the genetic diversity of these rare breeds, helping to ensure their survival. This aspect of designer dog breeding aligns with the values of responsible breeding and ethical practices, a topic of great importance in the dog breeding community.

The appeal of designer dogs extends beyond their physical traits. Their unique names and adorable appearances have also played a role in their popularity. Breeds like the Labradoodle, Cockapoo, and Schnoodle have become household names, recognized by dog enthusiasts across the globe. This recognition has led to increased demand for these crossbreeds, making them highly sought after among dog owners.

In conclusion, the appeal and popularity of designer dogs lie in their ability to combine the best qualities of two or more breeds, offering a wider range of options for dog owners with specific needs or preferences. These crossbreeds also contribute to the preservation of rare and endangered dog breeds, while their unique names and adorable appearances have made them widely recognized and sought after. Whether you are a small breed dog breeder, a service dog breeder, or simply a dog lover looking for a companion, designer dogs provide a delightful and fascinating option.

Understanding the Different Types of Designer Dogs

Chapter 4: Understanding the Different Types of Designer Dogs

Introduction:

In the world of dog breeding, there has been a growing trend of creating designer dogs through crossbreeding. These unique canines are the result of carefully planned breeding between two different purebred dogs. This chapter will provide an in-depth understanding of designer dogs, exploring their origins, characteristics, and the various types of designer breeds available today.

Section 1: What are Designer Dogs?

Designer dogs, also known as crossbreeds or hybrid dogs, are bred by intentionally mating two different purebred dogs. The goal is to combine the desirable traits of both parent breeds, resulting in a dog with a unique appearance, temperament, and health benefits. These dogs have gained popularity among dog owners due to their charming looks, hypoallergenic coats, and friendly personalities.

Section 2: Origins of Designer Dogs:

The concept of designer dogs originated in the late 20th century when breeders began experimenting with crossbreeding to create dogs with specific traits. The first designer dog, the Labradoodle, was bred in the 1980s, combining the intelligence of a Labrador Retriever with the hypoallergenic coat of a Poodle. Since then, numerous designer breeds have emerged, each with its own distinct characteristics.

Section 3: Types of Designer Dogs:

3.1 Small Breed Designer Dogs:

Small breed designer dogs, such as the Cockapoo (Cocker Spaniel + Poodle) or the Maltipoo (Maltese + Poodle), are ideal for individuals living in apartments or those seeking a companion that requires less exercise. These breeds often have low-shedding coats and are known for their affectionate nature.

3.2 Large Breed Designer Dogs:

For those looking for larger designer dogs, breeds like the Bernedoodle (Bernese Mountain Dog + Poodle) or the Goldendoodle (Golden Retriever + Poodle) are excellent choices. These dogs combine the loyalty and intelligence of their parent breeds while often having reduced shedding and hypoallergenic coats.

3.3 Designer Dogs for Special Needs Individuals:

Certain designer dog breeds, such as the Autism Assistance Dog (Golden Retriever + Poodle) or the Psychiatric Service Dog (Labrador Retriever + Poodle), are specifically bred to assist individuals with special needs. These dogs undergo specialized training to provide support and companionship.

Section 4: Responsible Breeding and Ethical Practices:

While the popularity of designer dogs continues to rise, it is essential to emphasize responsible breeding and ethical practices. Breeders should prioritize the health and well-being of the dogs, ensuring proper genetic testing, socialization, and veterinary care. Responsible breeders also carefully screen potential owners to ensure a good match between the dog and its future family.

Conclusion:

Understanding the different types of designer dogs allows dog owners to make informed decisions when choosing a new furry family member. Whether you desire a small, low-shedding companion or a larger, hypoallergenic working dog, designer breeds offer a wide range of options. However, it is crucial to support responsible breeders who prioritize the welfare of their dogs and adhere to ethical breeding practices.

The Controversies Surrounding Designer Dog Breeding

In recent years, the popularity of designer dogs has soared, with more and more dog owners seeking out these unique crossbreeds. However, this trend has not been without its fair share of controversies. Designer dog breeding, also known as crossbreeding, involves intentionally mating two different purebred dogs to create a new mixed breed. This practice has sparked debates among various dog breeding communities and animal welfare activists.

One of the main concerns surrounding designer dog breeding is the health and welfare of the resulting puppies. While some breeders claim that crossbreeding can produce healthier dogs by reducing the occurrence of genetic disorders, others argue that it can actually lead to an increase in health problems. The lack of genetic diversity in some designer dog breeds can result in inherited conditions such as hip dysplasia, heart disease, or even neurological disorders.

Another contentious issue is the ethics of designer dog breeding. Critics argue that intentionally creating mixed breed dogs for profit is unethical, as it contributes to the overpopulation of dogs in shelters and rescues. They believe that breeders should focus on responsible breeding practices, prioritizing the health and well-being of the dogs rather than meeting market demands for trendy crossbreeds.

Furthermore, there is ongoing debate about whether designer dogs should be considered as "purebred" or not. Some argue that these crossbreeds should not be recognized as legitimate breeds, as they do not conform to the breed standards and characteristics established for purebred dogs. This controversy has led to disputes within the dog show community and the reluctance of kennel clubs to accept designer dogs as official breeds.

Despite the controversies, it is important to recognize that not all designer dog breeders are unethical or neglectful of the welfare of their dogs. Responsible breeders prioritize health testing, socialization, and proper care for their breeding dogs and puppies. They strive to improve the breed and create healthy, well-rounded companions for dog owners.

As a dog owner, it is crucial to be informed and educated about the controversies surrounding designer dog breeding. By understanding the potential health risks and ethical concerns associated with these crossbreeds, you can make a more informed decision when choosing a dog. Additionally, supporting responsible breeders and adopting from shelters or rescues are alternatives that can help address the issues associated with designer dog breeding.

In conclusion, the controversies surrounding designer dog breeding continue to divide the dog breeding community and raise important questions about the ethics and welfare of these crossbreeds. As a responsible dog owner, it is essential to consider these concerns and make informed choices when it comes to selecting a new furry companion.

Chapter 2: Small Breed Dog Breeding

Characteristics and Traits of Small Breed Dogs

Small breed dogs are a popular choice among dog owners for various reasons. They are known for their adorable appearance, compact size, and friendly personalities. In this subchapter, we will explore the characteristics and traits that make small breed dogs unique and discuss how they differ from their larger counterparts.

One of the most notable characteristics of small breed dogs is their size. These dogs typically weigh less than 25 pounds and stand no taller than 16 inches at the shoulder. Their small size makes them more suitable for apartment living or for owners with limited space. Additionally, their compact size allows them to be easily transported and carried, making them ideal travel companions.

Small breed dogs are known for their energetic and lively personalities. They often have a lot of energy and require regular exercise to keep them happy and healthy. Despite their small size, they are often fearless and have a big personality. They are confident, alert, and make excellent watchdogs, alerting their owners to any potential threats.

Another characteristic of small breed dogs is their adaptability. They can thrive in various living situations, including both urban and rural environments. They are often well-suited for families with children, as they tend to be playful and enjoy spending time with their human companions. However, due to their small size, they may be more susceptible to injury, so caution should be taken when interacting with larger dogs or in high-energy situations.

Small breed dogs also have longer lifespans compared to larger breeds. While this can vary depending on the specific breed, small dogs generally live longer, with some reaching 15 years or more. This longevity allows for a longer companionship and more cherished memories with their owners.

In conclusion, small breed dogs possess a unique set of characteristics and traits that make them appealing to a wide range of dog owners. Their small size, energetic personalities, adaptability, and longer lifespans contribute to their popularity. Whether as a companion for individuals with special needs, a show dog, or a beloved family pet, small breed dogs bring joy and companionship to their owners while requiring responsible breeding and ethical practices to ensure their well-being.

Popular Small Breed Crossbreeds

Small breed crossbreeds have gained immense popularity among dog owners in recent years. These adorable canines are the result of carefully planned breeding between two different small dog breeds, creating unique combinations that appeal to a wide range of dog enthusiasts. In this subchapter, we will explore some of the most popular small breed crossbreeds and the traits that make them so sought after.

One of the most beloved small breed crossbreeds is the Cockapoo. This delightful mix between a Cocker Spaniel and a Poodle combines the intelligence and low-shedding coat of the Poodle with the friendly and affectionate nature of the Cocker Spaniel. Cockapoos are known for their playful personalities and make excellent family pets.

Another popular small breed crossbreed is the Shihpoo, a cross between a Shih Tzu and a Poodle. These small, hypoallergenic dogs are highly intelligent and make wonderful companions. Shihpoos are known for their loving nature and are often sought after by individuals with allergies due to their low-shedding coats.

The Cavachon is a crossbreed between a Cavalier King Charles Spaniel and a Bichon Frise. These small, fluffy dogs are incredibly friendly and gentle, making them perfect for families with children or individuals seeking a loyal and devoted companion. Cavachons are known for their playful nature and adaptability to various living situations.

Another popular choice is the Maltipoo, a cross between a Maltese and a Poodle. These adorable little dogs are highly intelligent and easy to train. Maltipoos are known for their affectionate and social nature, making them excellent therapy dogs or companions for individuals with special needs.

These are just a few examples of the many small breed crossbreeds available to dog enthusiasts. It is important to note that responsible breeding and ethical practices should always be upheld when considering crossbreeding. Dog owners and breeders alike should prioritize the health and well-being of the dogs, ensuring proper health testing and care.

Whether you are a small breed dog breeder, a purebred enthusiast, or someone interested in designer dogs, small breed crossbreeds offer a unique and exciting option. These adorable canines bring together the best traits of their parent breeds, resulting in loving, loyal, and highly adaptable companions. Explore the world of small breed crossbreeds and discover the perfect furry friend to enrich your life.

Breeding Considerations for Small Breed Dogs

When it comes to breeding small breed dogs, there are several important factors that dog owners and breeders need to consider. These considerations are crucial in ensuring the health, well-being, and longevity of these beloved canine companions. In this subchapter, we will delve into the unique aspects of small breed dog breeding and provide valuable insights for various niches within the dog breeding community.

Small breed dog breeding requires meticulous attention to detail due to the inherent fragility and specific needs of these dogs. One of the primary considerations is the size of the breeding pair. It is essential to select dogs that are within the appropriate size range to avoid complications during the breeding process and potential health issues for both the mother and the puppies.

Another crucial factor to consider is the genetic health of the breeding pair. Small breeds are often prone to certain genetic conditions such as patellar luxation, dental problems, and respiratory issues. Responsible breeders should thoroughly screen potential parents for these conditions to reduce the risk of passing them on to future generations. Regular health check-ups, genetic testing, and consultations with veterinarians are vital to ensuring the overall well-being of the breeding pair.

In addition to genetic health, temperament should also be carefully considered when breeding small dogs. Small breeds often possess distinctive personalities and temperaments, which can impact their suitability for certain niches such as service dog breeding or breeding for special needs individuals. It is essential to select breeding pairs with stable and trainable temperaments to produce puppies that can excel in these specific roles.

Ethical practices and responsible breeding are of utmost importance in small breed dog breeding. Breeders should be knowledgeable about the breed standards, adhere to ethical guidelines, and prioritize the welfare of the dogs above all else. It is crucial to provide proper care, nutrition, socialization, and a safe environment for the breeding dogs and their offspring.

By considering these breeding factors and practicing responsible and ethical breeding, small breed dog enthusiasts can contribute to the betterment of these beloved companions. Whether you are a breeder focusing on purebred dogs, designer crossbreeds, or working and service dogs, these considerations will help ensure the health, temperament, and overall quality of the puppies being produced.

Remember, breeding small breed dogs is a privilege and a responsibility. By upholding these standards, we can continue to enhance the lives of these remarkable canines and promote the values of responsible and ethical dog breeding.

Health Concerns and Genetic Testing in Small Breed Dog Breeding

As a dog owner and a small breed dog breeder, it is essential to be aware of the health concerns associated with breeding and the importance of genetic testing. In this subchapter, we will delve into the key health concerns in small breed dogs and the significance of genetic testing in the breeding process.

Small breed dogs are beloved for their compact size, adorable features, and unique personalities. However, they are often prone to specific health issues due to their genetic makeup. These health concerns can range from orthopedic problems like luxating patella and hip dysplasia to respiratory issues such as collapsed trachea and brachycephalic airway syndrome. Additionally, small breeds may be predisposed to dental problems, heart diseases, and certain types of cancer.

To ensure the well-being of future generations, small breed dog breeders must prioritize genetic testing. Genetic testing allows breeders to identify potential genetic disorders and make informed breeding decisions. By conducting tests for known genetic conditions, breeders can select breeding pairs that are less likely to produce offspring with these issues. This practice not only promotes healthier puppies but also contributes to the overall improvement of the breed.

Genetic testing can identify carriers, affected individuals, and clear dogs. Carriers have one copy of the faulty gene but do not exhibit symptoms, while affected individuals have two copies of the gene and may display the associated health condition. Clear dogs, on the other hand, do not possess the faulty gene at all. By selecting breeding dogs that are clear or have a lower risk of passing on genetic conditions, breeders can significantly reduce the prevalence of these health concerns in future litters.

Responsible breeding and ethical practices in small breed dog breeding also involve regular health screenings for potential breeding dogs. These screenings may include evaluations for hip and elbow dysplasia, eye diseases, and cardiac abnormalities. By prioritizing the health of their breeding dogs, breeders can improve the overall health of the breed and produce puppies that are less prone to inherited health problems.

In conclusion, as a dog owner and breeder, it is crucial to be aware of the health concerns associated with small breed dogs and the significance of genetic testing. By conducting genetic tests and health screenings, breeders can make informed decisions that promote the well-being of their breeding dogs and future generations. By prioritizing responsible breeding and ethical practices, we can ensure that small breed dogs thrive and continue to bring joy to our lives.

Chapter 3: Large Breed Dog Breeding

Characteristics and Traits of Large Breed Dogs

When it comes to dog breeds, size plays a significant role in determining their unique characteristics and traits. Large breed dogs, in particular, possess distinctive qualities that set them apart from their smaller counterparts. In this subchapter, we will explore the key traits of large breed dogs, shedding light on their specific needs, temperament, and suitability for various niches within the dog breeding community.

One of the characteristics that define large breed dogs is their imposing size. These dogs typically weigh 50 pounds or more and stand taller than 24 inches at the shoulder. Their large stature gives them a commanding presence, making them suitable for roles such as working dogs, show dogs, and service dogs.

In terms of temperament, large breed dogs often display a calm and composed demeanor. This makes them ideal for roles that require stability and reliability, such as police or search and rescue dogs. Large breeds are known for their loyalty and protective instincts, making them excellent companions and guardians for families and individuals with special needs.

Another important consideration with large breed dogs is their exercise and space requirements. Due to their size, these dogs need ample space to move around comfortably. Engaging in regular exercise is crucial to prevent obesity and maintain their overall health. Large breeds often excel in activities such as agility, obedience, and tracking.

When it comes to breeding large breed dogs, responsible and ethical practices are essential. Breeders should prioritize the health and well-being of the dogs, ensuring that they are free from genetic disorders commonly associated with larger breeds. Regular health screenings, including hip and elbow evaluations, should be conducted to minimize the risk of hereditary diseases.

Furthermore, large breed dog breeding requires careful consideration of potential owners. These dogs are not suitable for everyone due to their size and exercise needs. Responsible breeders should educate prospective owners about the specific requirements of large breeds, helping them make informed decisions and providing ongoing support.

In conclusion, large breed dogs possess unique characteristics and traits that make them stand out in the dog breeding community. Their imposing size, calm temperament, and loyalty make them well-suited for various roles such as working dogs, show dogs, and service dogs. However, responsible breeding and ethical practices are crucial to ensure the health and well-being of these magnificent canines and to match them with suitable owners who can meet their specific needs.

Popular Large Breed Crossbreeds

Crossbreeding has gained popularity in recent years, as dog owners seek to combine the best characteristics of different breeds into one unique and lovable companion. In this subchapter, we will explore some of the most popular large breed crossbreeds that have captured the hearts of dog owners around the world.

1. Labradoodle: This cross between a Labrador Retriever and a Poodle has become one of the most sought-after large breed crossbreeds. Labradoodles are known for their intelligence, friendly nature, and hypoallergenic coats, making them a perfect choice for families with allergies.

2. Goldendoodle: Combining the Golden Retriever and the Poodle, the Goldendoodle is loved for its friendly and affectionate personality. These crossbreeds are often used as therapy and assistance dogs due to their gentle nature and high trainability.

3. Bernedoodle: Mixing the Bernese Mountain Dog with a Poodle results in the Bernedoodle, a large breed crossbreed that is known for its intelligence and loyalty. Bernedoodles are highly adaptable and make excellent family pets.

4. Sheepadoodle: A cross between an Old English Sheepdog and a Poodle, Sheepadoodles are prized for their hypoallergenic coats and gentle temperament. These crossbreeds are often seen as both loving family pets and reliable working dogs.

5. Saint Berdoodle: Combining the Saint Bernard and the Poodle, the Saint Berdoodle is a gentle giant known for its loyalty and friendly nature. These large breed crossbreeds make excellent therapy dogs and are cherished by families who appreciate their calm and patient demeanor.

6. Daniff: The Daniff is a mix between the Great Dane and the Mastiff, resulting in a large and powerful crossbreed. Known for their protective instincts and gentle nature, Daniffs are often used as working dogs in search and rescue operations.

7. Boxerdoodle: A mix between the Boxer and the Poodle, Boxerdoodles are energetic and playful crossbreeds. These large breed dogs are loved for their loyalty and trainability, making them suitable for various purposes, including as service dogs.

These popular large breed crossbreeds offer dog owners the opportunity to enjoy the best qualities of different breeds in one unique companion. However, it is essential to remember that responsible breeding and ethical practices should always be followed to ensure the health and well-being of these beloved dogs.

Breeding Considerations for Large Breed Dogs

When it comes to breeding large breed dogs, there are several important considerations that every responsible breeder should keep in mind. Large breeds, such as Great Danes, Saint Bernards, and Mastiffs, have unique needs and potential health issues that must be taken into account to ensure the well-being of both the parent dogs and their future offspring.

First and foremost, it is crucial to select breeding pairs that are free from genetic disorders commonly seen in large breeds. This requires thorough health screenings and testing for conditions like hip and elbow dysplasia, heart disease, and certain types of cancers. By choosing dogs with clean bill of health, you can minimize the risk of passing on these hereditary conditions to future generations.

Another consideration is the size and structure of the parent dogs. Large breeds often have specific physical characteristics that need to be taken into account during the breeding process. For example, it is important to avoid pairing dogs with extreme body shapes or disproportionate sizes, as this can lead to structural issues and problems with mobility in the offspring.

Temperament is also a crucial factor to consider when breeding large breed dogs. It is essential to select breeding pairs with stable and even temperaments, as these traits are highly desirable in family pets. Aggression or excessive fearfulness should be avoided to ensure that the puppies grow up to be well-adjusted and confident dogs.

Additionally, proper nutrition and exercise play a significant role in the development and overall health of large breed dogs. Breeding pairs should be fed a balanced diet that meets their specific nutritional needs, taking into account their size and activity levels. Regular exercise and mental stimulation are also vital to prevent obesity and promote a healthy lifestyle for the parent dogs.

Lastly, it is essential to have a solid understanding of the demand and purpose for large breed dogs. Whether you are breeding for show, work, or companionship, it is crucial to consider the needs and preferences of potential owners. Understanding the market and the requirements of different niches will help you breed dogs that are not only physically sound but also suited for their intended roles.

In conclusion, breeding large breed dogs requires careful consideration and attention to various factors. By selecting healthy breeding pairs, paying attention to physical structure and temperament, providing proper nutrition and exercise, and understanding the market demand, you can contribute to the production of well-rounded and healthy large breed dogs that bring joy and companionship to dog owners across various niches.

Health Concerns and Genetic Testing in Large Breed Dog Breeding

As a dog owner, it is essential to be aware of the potential health concerns associated with breeding large breed dogs. Genetic testing plays a crucial role in identifying and preventing these issues, ensuring the overall well-being of the dogs and their offspring. In this subchapter, we will explore the importance of genetic testing in large breed dog breeding and its implications for various niches in the dog breeding community.

Large breed dogs, such as Great Danes, Saint Bernards, and Mastiffs, are prone to certain genetic health conditions. These can include hip dysplasia, elbow dysplasia, heart disease, and certain types of cancer. By conducting genetic testing, breeders can identify if their dogs carry any of these genetic diseases, allowing them to make informed breeding decisions and reduce the risk of passing these conditions onto future generations.

For small breed dog breeders, understanding the health concerns in large breed dogs can provide valuable insights when crossing them with smaller breeds. By selecting a smaller breed that is genetically healthier, breeders can potentially mitigate the risk of passing on health issues to the offspring.

Designer dog breeders, who create crossbreeds by combining two different breeds, must also prioritize genetic testing. By testing both parent breeds, breeders can identify any potential health concerns and determine the compatibility of the parent breeds regarding genetic health. This ensures that the resulting crossbreed has a reduced risk of inheriting genetic diseases from either parent.

Purebred dog breeders, rare breed dog breeders, and show dog breeders should also prioritize genetic testing to maintain breed standards and overall health. By identifying and excluding dogs with genetic health issues from their breeding programs, breeders can work towards producing healthier and genetically diverse litters.

Working dog breeders, such as those breeding police or search and rescue dogs, must ensure the physical and mental well-being of their dogs. Genetic testing helps identify potential health concerns that may hinder a dog's performance or longevity in these demanding roles.

Service dog breeders, responsible for breeding therapy or assistance dogs, should prioritize genetic testing to ensure the long-term health and suitability of their dogs for their intended tasks. By selecting dogs with a lower risk of genetic diseases, breeders can increase the chances of producing reliable and healthy service dogs.

Lastly, breeders involved in breeding and selling puppies for special needs individuals must prioritize genetic testing to ensure that the puppies they provide have the best chance of leading healthy lives. This involves testing for conditions that might impact a dog's ability to fulfill their role as a companion or assistance animal.

In summary, genetic testing is a vital tool in large breed dog breeding. By prioritizing genetic health and responsible breeding practices, breeders can work towards producing healthier and genetically diverse litters. This not only ensures the well-being of the dogs but also contributes to the overall improvement and longevity of various dog breeds and crossbreeds.

Chapter 4: Designer Dog Breeding (Crossbreeds)

Understanding the Concept of Crossbreeding

Crossbreeding is a fascinating concept in the world of dog breeding. It involves breeding two different purebred dogs to create a new and unique hybrid, known as a designer dog. This subchapter aims to provide dog owners, including those involved in small breed dog breeding, large breed dog breeding, designer dog breeding, purebred dog breeding, rare breed dog breeding, show dog breeding, working dog breeding, service dog breeding, breeding and selling puppies for special needs individuals, as well as those interested in responsible breeding and ethical practices, with a comprehensive understanding of crossbreeding.

Crossbreeding offers numerous benefits to both the breeder and the dog owner. By combining the desirable traits of two specific breeds, such as intelligence, temperament, and physical characteristics, breeders can create a dog that possesses the best qualities of both parent breeds. This allows for a wider range of options and variety in the dog breeding world.

For dog owners, crossbreeding can provide a unique and specialized companion. Designer dogs are often bred to serve specific purposes, such as therapy or assistance dogs, and can be tailored to meet the needs of individuals with special requirements. Additionally, crossbreeds tend to have fewer health issues compared to purebred dogs, as they benefit from increased genetic diversity.

It is important to note that responsible breeding and ethical practices should always be the foundation of any crossbreeding program. Breeders must prioritize the health and well-being of their dogs above all else. This includes conducting health tests on parent dogs to ensure they are free from genetic diseases that may be present in their respective breeds.

Furthermore, it is crucial to educate potential dog owners about the advantages and challenges of owning a crossbred dog. Each designer dog breed is unique and may require specific care and training. Prospective owners should be well-informed about the characteristics and needs of the chosen crossbreed to ensure a successful and fulfilling companionship.

In conclusion, understanding the concept of crossbreeding is essential for dog breeders and owners alike. This subchapter has provided an overview of the benefits, considerations, and responsible practices associated with crossbreeding. By embracing the art of crossbreeding canines, breeders can create new breeds that cater to the diverse needs and preferences of dog owners in various niches.

Popular Designer Dog Crossbreeds

Designer dog crossbreeds have become increasingly popular among dog owners in recent years. These unique and adorable canines are the result of carefully planned breeding between two different purebred dogs, resulting in a new hybrid breed that combines the best traits of both parents. In this subchapter, we will explore some of the most popular designer dog crossbreeds and the reasons behind their growing popularity.

One of the most well-known designer dog crossbreeds is the Labradoodle, which combines the intelligence and trainability of the Labrador Retriever with the hypoallergenic coat of the Poodle. This makes Labradoodles an excellent choice for families with allergies or those who want a low-shedding dog. These friendly and energetic dogs are often used as therapy or assistance dogs due to their gentle nature.

Another popular crossbreed is the Goldendoodle, a mix between a Golden Retriever and a Poodle. With their friendly and outgoing personalities, Goldendoodles are beloved by families and individuals alike. They are known for their intelligence, loyalty, and hypoallergenic coats, making them an ideal choice for those with allergies or asthma.

The Cockapoo is a crossbreed between a Cocker Spaniel and a Poodle. These small and affectionate dogs are known for their playful and loving nature. Cockapoos are great companions for families and individuals, and their low-shedding coat makes them a popular choice for people with allergies.

If you're looking for a smaller designer dog crossbreed, the Maltipoo might be the perfect choice. This mix between a Maltese and a Poodle is known for its friendly and outgoing personality. Maltipoos are often sought after for their hypoallergenic coats and small size, making them suitable for apartment living.

It's important to note that while designer dog crossbreeds have gained popularity, responsible breeding and ethical practices should always be followed. Breeders should prioritize the health and well-being of the dogs, ensuring that both parents are healthy and genetically tested. Additionally, potential owners should do thorough research and consider the specific needs and characteristics of the crossbreed they are interested in.

In conclusion, designer dog crossbreeds have captured the hearts of dog owners around the world. These unique and wonderful hybrids offer a combination of desirable traits from different purebred dogs, making them excellent companions for various lifestyles and needs. Whether you're considering a Labradoodle, Goldendoodle, Cockapoo, or Maltipoo, remember to choose a responsible breeder and provide a loving and caring home for your new furry friend.

Breeding Considerations for Designer Dogs

Introduction:

Breeding designer dogs, also known as crossbreeding canines, has gained popularity among dog owners in recent years. These unique and often adorable combinations of two different purebred dogs offer an exciting alternative to traditional breeds. However, before embarking on the journey of designer dog breeding, there are several important considerations that dog owners should keep in mind. This subchapter will delve into the breeding considerations for designer dogs, addressing the various niches within the dog breeding community.

1. Health and Genetics:

When breeding designer dogs, it is crucial to prioritize the health and genetics of both parent breeds. Conduct thorough health screenings, including genetic testing, to ensure that potential health issues are minimized in the offspring. By selecting healthy parent dogs, you can increase the chances of producing healthy and resilient designer puppies.

2. Temperament and Behavior:

Consider the temperament and behavior of the parent breeds to ensure that the designer puppies inherit desirable traits. Assess the compatibility of the two breeds, as some combinations may result in conflicting temperaments. For example, while one breed may be known for its friendly nature, the other may possess protective instincts. It is essential to strike a balance to create well-rounded and suitable companions.

3. Size and Exercise Requirements:

Designer dogs can vary significantly in size, ranging from small to large breeds. Consider the space available in your home and the exercise requirements of the parent breeds. Some designer dogs may require more physical activity, while others may be content with less exercise. Understanding these needs will help match the puppies to suitable owners.

4. Purpose and Niche Breeding:

Different breeds serve different purposes, such as show dogs, working dogs, service dogs, or companions for individuals with special needs. Identify the niche you wish to target and select parent breeds accordingly. For example, if you aim to breed service dogs, select parent breeds known for their intelligence, trainability, and calm temperament.

5. Responsible Breeding Practices:

As a designer dog breeder, it is essential to adhere to responsible breeding practices and ethical guidelines. This includes providing proper nutrition, veterinary care, and socialization for both parent dogs and puppies. Avoid overbreeding and ensure that each breeding pair receives adequate rest between litters. Additionally, educate potential owners about the responsibilities of dog ownership and the specific needs of designer dogs.

Conclusion:

Breeding designer dogs can be a rewarding experience for dog owners involved in various niches of the dog breeding community. By considering the health, genetics, temperament, size, purpose, and responsible breeding practices, you can contribute to the development of well-balanced and healthy designer puppies. As the popularity of designer dogs continues to grow, it is crucial to prioritize the welfare and well-being of these unique crossbreeds.

Health Concerns and Genetic Testing in Designer Dog Breeding

As dog owners, we often prioritize the health and well-being of our beloved pets. When it comes to designer dog breeding, however, there are unique considerations that must be taken into account. In this subchapter, we will explore the health concerns associated with designer dog breeding and the importance of genetic testing in ensuring the well-being of these crossbred canines.

Small breed dog breeding, large breed dog breeding, and designer dog breeding all present their own set of health concerns. While small breeds may be prone to dental issues and patellar luxation, large breeds are susceptible to hip dysplasia and certain types of cancer. Designer dogs, being a combination of two or more breeds, may inherit health issues from both parent breeds. It is crucial for breeders to be aware of these potential health concerns and take appropriate measures to minimize their impact on the offspring.

Genetic testing plays a crucial role in identifying and addressing health concerns in designer dog breeding. By analyzing the DNA of parent dogs, breeders can determine the likelihood of passing on genetic disorders to their offspring. This allows breeders to make informed decisions and select mating pairs that are less likely to produce puppies with inherited diseases or conditions. Genetic testing also helps in identifying carriers of certain genetic disorders, which can be useful in avoiding pairing two carriers and potentially producing affected puppies.

In addition to genetic testing, responsible breeding and ethical practices play a vital role in promoting the health of designer dogs. Breeders should prioritize the overall well-being of their dogs, providing them with proper nutrition, regular exercise, and regular veterinary care. It is also important to maintain a clean and safe breeding environment to prevent the spread of diseases and infections.

For breeders involved in show dog breeding, working dog breeding, or service dog breeding, the health concerns in designer dog breeding become even more critical. These dogs may be subjected to rigorous physical demands, and any underlying health issues can impact their performance and overall quality of life. Breeders should prioritize genetic testing and ensure that their dogs are fit for the specific tasks they are bred for.

In conclusion, health concerns and genetic testing are of utmost importance in designer dog breeding. By being aware of potential health issues, conducting genetic testing, and practicing responsible breeding, breeders can ensure the well-being of their designer dogs and promote ethical practices in the breeding community. As dog owners, it is our responsibility to support and encourage breeders who prioritize the health and happiness of their dogs.

Chapter 5: Purebred Dog Breeding

The Importance of Preserving Purebred Dog Breeds

In the world of dog breeding, the concept of crossbreeding canines has gained immense popularity in recent years. Many dog owners are enticed by the allure of designer dogs, which are a result of crossing two purebred breeds. While crossbreeds indeed possess unique characteristics, it is crucial not to overlook the importance of preserving purebred dog breeds.

For small breed dog breeding enthusiasts, preserving purebred dog breeds ensures the continuation of traits specific to these breeds. Whether it's the feisty nature of a Chihuahua or the affectionate demeanor of a Shih Tzu, purebred dogs have distinct qualities that attract dog lovers. By preserving these breeds, we ensure that future generations can experience and enjoy the unique characteristics that make each breed special.

Similarly, large breed dog breeding requires a focus on preserving purebred breeds. The strength, loyalty, and protective nature of breeds like the German Shepherd or the Great Dane are highly valued by many dog owners. These breeds have been carefully developed over generations to possess specific traits that make them excellent working or family dogs. Preserving the purity of these breeds guarantees that their exceptional qualities will endure.

For those involved in designer dog breeding, understanding the importance of preserving purebred dog breeds is essential. Crossbreeds are undoubtedly popular, but they are reliant on the existence of their purebred parent breeds. By preserving the purity of these breeds, we ensure a steady supply of healthy and genetically diverse dogs that can be used to create new and exciting crossbreeds.

Moreover, purebred dog breeds play a vital role in various specialized areas of dog breeding. Show dog breeding relies on the preservation of specific breed standards to showcase the best representatives of each breed. Working dog breeding, including police and search and rescue dogs, requires purebred breeds with specific physical and behavioral traits. Service dog breeding for therapy or assistance purposes also benefits from the preservation of purebred dog breeds.

Lastly, responsible breeding and ethical practices in dog breeding necessitate the preservation of purebred dog breeds. By focusing on maintaining the health, temperament, and genetic diversity of purebred dogs, breeders can ensure the overall well-being of future generations. Responsible breeding practices include health testing, genetic screenings, and careful selection of breeding pairs to prevent the propagation of hereditary diseases.

In conclusion, while the allure of designer dogs and crossbreeds cannot be denied, it is crucial to remember the importance of preserving purebred dog breeds. From small to large breeds, show dogs to working dogs, and service dogs to rare breeds, each category benefits from the preservation of purebred dogs. By appreciating and safeguarding the unique qualities of purebred breeds, we ensure a future filled with healthy, diverse, and exceptional canines for generations to come.

Breeding Strategies for Purebred Dogs

Breeding purebred dogs requires careful planning and consideration to ensure the health, temperament, and overall quality of the offspring. In this subchapter, we will explore various breeding strategies that can be applied to different niches within the dog breeding community, including small breed dog breeding, large breed dog breeding, designer dog breeding, rare breed dog breeding, show dog breeding, working dog breeding, service dog breeding, breeding for special needs individuals, and responsible breeding practices.

For small breed dog breeding, it is important to focus on maintaining the breed's unique characteristics while also minimizing health issues that are common in small dogs. Selecting breeding pairs with good overall health, proper conformation, and sound temperament is crucial. Additionally, considering the size and weight of the dogs is essential to avoid complications during the birthing process.

In large breed dog breeding, the emphasis should be on producing dogs with excellent structure and soundness. Breeding pairs should be chosen based on their temperament, health clearances, and working abilities if applicable. Furthermore, it is important to be aware of potential genetic issues that may be prevalent in certain large breeds and take steps to avoid them through selective breeding.

Designer dog breeding involves the intentional crossing of two purebred dogs to create a new breed. The focus here is on combining desirable traits from both parent breeds, such as hypoallergenic coats or specific temperaments. Careful consideration should be given to the health and compatibility of the parent breeds to ensure the well-being of the crossbred puppies.

Rare breed dog breeding requires a deep understanding of the breed's history, characteristics, and genetic diversity. Breeding pairs should be carefully selected to preserve the breed's unique qualities, prevent inbreeding, and maintain a healthy gene pool. Collaborating with other breeders and organizations dedicated to rare breed preservation can be beneficial in this niche.

For show dog breeding, the main goal is to produce puppies that conform to breed standards and excel in the show ring. Breeding pairs should possess exceptional qualities, including proper conformation, temperament, and movement. Consulting experienced show dog breeders and participating in dog shows can provide valuable insights into the breeding process.

Working dog breeding, such as police or search and rescue dogs, focuses on producing canines with high intelligence, drive, and physical abilities. Breeding pairs should have proven working abilities, health clearances, and stable temperaments. Collaboration with professionals in the working dog field can help ensure the offspring's suitability for their intended roles.

Service dog breeding involves producing dogs that excel in providing assistance and therapy to individuals with special needs. Breeding pairs should possess the desired traits for service work, such as trainability, calmness, and empathy. Cooperation with service dog organizations and trainers can contribute to the success of such breeding programs.

When breeding for special needs individuals, it is essential to consider the specific requirements of the individual and their potential dog. Breeding pairs should be selected based on their health clearances, temperament, and compatibility with special needs individuals. Ensuring the puppies receive appropriate training and socialization is crucial in providing the best possible match.

Lastly, responsible breeding practices should always align with ethical standards. This includes prioritizing the health and welfare of both the parent dogs and the puppies, conducting proper health screenings, providing adequate care, and finding suitable homes for the puppies. Responsible breeders also strive to educate potential owners about the breed's specific needs and responsibilities that come with dog ownership.

By understanding the different breeding strategies and tailoring them to specific niches, dog breeders can contribute to the betterment of purebred dogs and meet the diverse needs of dog owners across various areas of interest.

Health Concerns and Genetic Testing in Purebred Dog Breeding

Introduction:

When it comes to purebred dog breeding, there are various health concerns that breeders need to be aware of and address to ensure the well-being of their dogs. Genetic testing plays a crucial role in identifying potential health issues and enabling breeders to make informed decisions. This subchapter aims to shed light on the importance of genetic testing in purebred dog breeding and how it can contribute to responsible breeding and ethical practices.

1. Understanding Health Concerns in Purebred Dogs:

Purebred dogs are susceptible to certain genetic disorders due to their limited gene pool. Breeders must be familiar with the health concerns associated with their specific breed and take necessary precautions to prevent or minimize these issues. Common health concerns can include hip dysplasia, eye disorders, heart conditions, and various hereditary diseases.

2. The Role of Genetic Testing:

Genetic testing has revolutionized the field of dog breeding, providing breeders with valuable insights into their dog's genetic makeup. By conducting genetic tests, breeders can identify potential carriers of hereditary diseases, assess the risk of passing on these diseases to offspring, and make informed breeding decisions.

3. Benefits of Genetic Testing:

a) Disease Prevention: By identifying carriers of specific diseases, breeders can avoid breeding two carriers together, reducing the risk of offspring inheriting these diseases.

b) Improved Health: Genetic testing allows breeders to select breeding pairs that are less likely to produce offspring with health issues, ultimately improving the overall health of the breed.

c) Ethical Breeding: By prioritizing genetic testing, breeders demonstrate their commitment to producing healthy puppies and contribute to the long-term welfare of the breed.

4. Responsible Breeding Practices:

a) Collaboration with Veterinarians and Geneticists: Breeders should work closely with veterinary professionals and geneticists to ensure accurate and reliable genetic testing. Regular consultations can help breeders stay updated on the latest advancements in genetic testing and breeding practices.

b) Transparency and Education: Responsible breeders should be transparent about the health concerns associated with their breed and educate potential buyers about these issues. This helps ensure that future dog owners are well-informed and prepared to provide appropriate care for their pets.

Conclusion:

Genetic testing is an invaluable tool in purebred dog breeding that enables breeders to identify and address potential health concerns. By prioritizing genetic testing and responsible breeding practices, breeders can contribute to the overall health and well-being of their dogs while promoting ethical practices in the breeding community.

Chapter 6: Rare Breed Dog Breeding

Recognizing and Appreciating Rare Dog Breeds

In the world of dog breeding, there are countless breeds that have captured the hearts of dog owners across the globe. From popular breeds like Labradors and German Shepherds to lesser-known ones, each breed brings its own unique qualities and characteristics. However, there is a special group of dogs that deserves recognition and appreciation - the rare dog breeds.

Rare dog breeds are those that have a small population and are not commonly seen or recognized by the general public. These breeds often have a fascinating history and are known for their distinct physical features, temperaments, or working abilities. While they may not be as well-known as their more popular counterparts, they offer a charm and uniqueness that cannot be found elsewhere.

Appreciating and preserving rare dog breeds is vital to maintaining the diversity and health of the canine population. By recognizing these breeds, we can help ensure that their unique traits and genetics are preserved for future generations. It is through responsible breeding practices that we can prevent these rare breeds from disappearing altogether.

For small breed dog breeders, recognizing and appreciating rare breeds can open up new opportunities. By adding a rare breed to your breeding program, you can offer something different to potential owners who may be looking for a unique companion. Similarly, large breed dog breeders can explore rare breeds that possess impressive size, strength, and working abilities.

Designer dog breeders can also benefit from recognizing and appreciating rare breeds. By incorporating rare breeds into your crossbreeding programs, you can create extraordinary designer dogs that combine the best traits of multiple breeds. This can attract the attention of dog lovers who desire a one-of-a-kind companion.

Moreover, recognizing and appreciating rare breeds is of great importance for show, working, and service dog breeders. By diversifying the gene pool, these breeders can enhance the overall health and performance of their dogs. Rare breeds often have unique skills and talents that can be harnessed in various fields, such as search and rescue or therapy work.

Regardless of the niche you belong to as a breeder, recognizing and appreciating rare breeds is a testament to your commitment to responsible and ethical practices. It shows that you value the preservation of diversity in the dog breeding community and are dedicated to maintaining the well-being of these remarkable breeds.

In conclusion, recognizing and appreciating rare dog breeds is essential for dog owners and breeders alike. By shedding light on these unique breeds, we can ensure their preservation, contribute to the diversity of the dog population, and offer dog lovers a chance to experience the joy of owning a truly rare and special companion.

Breeding Considerations for Rare Dog Breeds

When it comes to breeding rare dog breeds, there are several important considerations that every responsible breeder should keep in mind. These considerations apply to dog owners and breeders of various niches, including small breed dog breeding, large breed dog breeding, designer dog breeding, purebred dog breeding, rare breed dog breeding, show dog breeding, working dog breeding, service dog breeding, breeding and selling puppies for special needs individuals, as well as responsible breeding and ethical practices in dog breeding.

First and foremost, it is crucial to understand the unique characteristics and needs of the rare breed you are working with. Rare dog breeds often have specific health issues or temperament traits that need to be carefully managed. Conduct thorough research and consult with experts to gather as much information as possible about the breed's history, genetic predispositions, and any potential health concerns.

When breeding rare dog breeds, genetic diversity is of utmost importance. Due to their limited population size, rare breeds often suffer from a lack of genetic variation, which can lead to increased susceptibility to inherited diseases. It is essential to work with a wide gene pool and avoid inbreeding to maintain the health and vitality of the breed.

Finding suitable breeding partners for rare breeds can be challenging, but it is crucial to prioritize quality over quantity. Look for dogs that complement each other in terms of health, temperament, and conformation. Conduct thorough health screenings and genetic testing to ensure that the breeding pair does not carry any inherited diseases that could be passed down to their offspring.

Responsible breeders of rare dog breeds should prioritize the wellbeing of their dogs. This includes providing proper nutrition, regular veterinary care, and an appropriate living environment. Breeding should only be done when both the male and female dogs are in optimal health and condition.

Lastly, it is essential for breeders of rare dog breeds to maintain open and transparent communication with other breeders and enthusiasts. Sharing knowledge, experiences, and genetic information can help in preserving and improving rare breeds. Participating in breed clubs, shows, and events can also contribute to the promotion and recognition of rare dog breeds.

In conclusion, breeding rare dog breeds requires careful consideration and a commitment to preserving the breed's health and vitality. By prioritizing genetic diversity, finding suitable breeding partners, and maintaining a focus on the overall well-being of the dogs, breeders can contribute to the preservation and improvement of rare breeds.

Health Concerns and Genetic Testing in Rare Breed Dog Breeding

As a dog owner, you are likely familiar with the joy and companionship that comes with having a furry friend by your side. Whether you are involved in small breed dog breeding, large breed dog breeding, designer dog breeding, purebred dog breeding, or any other niche within the dog breeding community, it is crucial to be aware of the health concerns that can arise and the role that genetic testing plays in ensuring the well-being of your beloved canines.

Rare breed dog breeding presents unique challenges when it comes to health concerns. Due to their limited population size, rare breeds often have a higher risk of inheriting certain genetic disorders. By understanding and addressing these potential health issues, breeders can work towards producing healthier offspring and preserving these rare breeds for generations to come.

Genetic testing plays a vital role in rare breed dog breeding. It allows breeders to identify potential genetic disorders that may be present within their breeding lines. By screening for these disorders, breeders can make informed decisions about which dogs to breed, minimizing the risk of passing on harmful genetic traits.

In addition to genetic testing, responsible breeders should also focus on maintaining a comprehensive health testing program. This includes regular check-ups, vaccinations, and screening for common health issues specific to their breed. By staying up-to-date with the latest research and advancements in veterinary medicine, breeders can ensure the overall health and well-being of their dogs.

Furthermore, ethical practices in dog breeding extend beyond health concerns. Breeders should prioritize the overall welfare of their dogs, providing them with appropriate living conditions, socialization, and mental stimulation. Responsible breeders also strive to promote responsible pet ownership and work to prevent the overpopulation of dogs by spaying or neutering puppies before they go to their new homes.

By prioritizing the health concerns of their dogs and implementing genetic testing protocols, breeders can contribute to the betterment of their chosen breeds. Whether you are involved in rare breed dog breeding, show dog breeding, or breeding for service or special needs individuals, it is essential to approach breeding with a commitment to responsible practices and the highest standards of care.

In conclusion, the health concerns and genetic testing in rare breed dog breeding are crucial aspects that every dog owner and breeder should be aware of. By understanding the potential risks, implementing genetic testing protocols, and embracing responsible breeding practices, you can contribute to the long-term health and well-being of your dogs and the preservation of rare breeds.

Chapter 7: Show Dog Breeding

The World of Dog Shows and Conformation Standards

Dog shows are not just a fun event for dog owners and enthusiasts; they play a significant role in the world of dog breeding. In this subchapter, we will explore the fascinating world of dog shows and the importance of conformation standards in breeding top-quality dogs.

Dog shows are competitions where purebred dogs are judged according to specific standards set by kennel clubs around the world. These standards outline the ideal characteristics, appearance, and temperament for each breed. Judges evaluate the dogs based on their adherence to these standards and award prizes accordingly.

For small breed dog breeders, dog shows are a valuable platform to showcase their carefully bred dogs. It allows them to compare their dogs against other top-quality specimens and gauge their breeding program's success. Similarly, large breed dog breeders can use dog shows to highlight the impressive size, strength, and structure of their dogs.

Designer dog breeders, who specialize in crossbreeds, can also participate in dog shows. These breeders aim to create unique and desirable combinations of two or more breeds. Dog shows provide them with an opportunity to demonstrate the positive traits they have achieved through careful selection and breeding.

In addition to breeders, dog shows are essential for owners of rare breeds. These breeds are often on the verge of extinction, and dog shows help raise awareness about their existence and encourage responsible breeding practices. Showcasing rare breeds at dog shows increases their visibility and encourages breed enthusiasts to take an interest in their preservation.

For breeders involved in working or service dog breeding, dog shows offer a chance to prove the dogs' abilities and suitability for their respective roles. Judges assess these dogs' working capabilities, such as obedience, agility, and temperament, in addition to their conformation.

It is vital to note that responsible breeding and ethical practices are at the heart of dog shows. Breeders who adhere to these principles prioritize the health, well-being, and genetic diversity of the dogs they breed. Dog shows promote responsible breeding by rewarding dogs that not only meet conformation standards but also display excellent overall health and sound temperament.

In conclusion, dog shows and conformation standards play a crucial role in the world of dog breeding. They provide breeders and owners with a platform to showcase their dogs, compare them against others, and contribute to the preservation of various breeds. Regardless of the niche one belongs to in the world of dog breeding, participating in dog shows can be a rewarding experience that promotes responsible breeding practices and celebrates the beauty and diversity of dogs.

Breeding Strategies for Show Dogs

Breeding show dogs requires a meticulous approach to ensure that the desired traits are passed down to future generations. In this subchapter, we will delve into the various strategies that can be employed by dog breeders to produce top-quality show dogs. Whether you are breeding small breeds, large breeds, purebreds, or designer dogs, these strategies are essential to achieve success in the show ring.

To begin with, it is crucial to have a clear understanding of the breed standards for show dogs. Each breed has specific characteristics that judges look for in the ring, such as conformation, coat color, size, and temperament. By familiarizing yourself with these standards, you can make informed decisions when selecting breeding pairs.

In show dog breeding, it is essential to prioritize health and genetic diversity. This means conducting thorough health screenings and genetic testing to identify any potential hereditary issues that may be present in the bloodline. Breeding dogs with sound health and diverse genetic backgrounds reduces the risk of passing on genetic disorders and enhances the overall health of the offspring.

Another important strategy is to carefully select the breeding pairs. Look for dogs that complement each other in terms of conformation and temperament. Studying pedigrees and lineage can provide valuable insights into the genetic strengths and weaknesses of potential breeding dogs. Choosing dogs with proven track records in the show ring or those from reputable breeders can greatly increase the chances of producing show-worthy offspring.

Consistency is key in show dog breeding. It is advisable to maintain a breeding program that focuses on producing consistent traits and characteristics across generations. This can be achieved by selectively breeding dogs that possess the desired traits and eliminating those that do not meet the standards.

Additionally, networking with other breeders and participating in dog shows and competitions can provide valuable exposure and knowledge. Attending seminars and workshops on breeding strategies can keep you updated with the latest advancements in the field.

Lastly, ethical practices and responsible breeding should always be the guiding principles. Prioritize the health and well-being of the dogs, and never compromise on their welfare for the sake of producing show-winning offspring. Ensure proper socialization, nutrition, and veterinary care for the breeding dogs and their puppies.

Breeding show dogs is an art that requires dedication, knowledge, and a deep passion for the breed. By implementing effective breeding strategies and adhering to ethical practices, you can contribute to the improvement of the breed and produce exceptional show dogs that bring joy and pride to their owners.

Training and Conditioning Show Dogs for Success

Introduction:

In the world of dog breeding, show dogs hold a special place. These dogs are not only bred for their physical attributes but also for their ability to perform in the show ring. To ensure that your show dog stands out from the competition, it is crucial to provide them with the right training and conditioning. In this subchapter, we will explore the various techniques and strategies that can help you train and condition your show dog for success.

Training:

Training plays a vital role in shaping a show dog's behavior and performance. It is essential to start training your show dog from a young age. Basic obedience commands such as sit, stay, and heel should be mastered before moving on to more advanced training techniques. Consistency, positive reinforcement, and patience are key when it comes to training show dogs.

One crucial aspect of training show dogs is teaching them to perform specific show ring behaviors. This includes gaiting, stacking, and presenting themselves to the judges. Show dogs should also be comfortable with being examined by strangers and standing still for long periods. Training techniques such as clicker training and shaping can be used to teach these behaviors effectively.

Conditioning:

Physical conditioning is equally important for show dogs. A well-conditioned dog not only looks impressive but also performs better in the show ring. Regular exercise, a balanced diet, and proper grooming are the cornerstones of conditioning show dogs.

Exercise should be tailored to suit the specific breed and individual dog. This can include daily walks, agility training, and even swimming. Regular exercise helps to build muscle tone, improve stamina, and maintain a healthy weight.

Diet plays a significant role in a show dog's overall health and appearance. Consult with a veterinarian or a canine nutritionist to develop a diet plan that meets your show dog's specific nutritional needs. A high-quality diet, rich in essential nutrients, will contribute to a show dog's coat quality, muscle development, and overall vitality.

Proper grooming is essential to maintain a show dog's appearance. Regular brushing, bathing, and nail trimming should be part of the grooming routine. Additionally, show dogs may require professional grooming to ensure they look their best in the show ring.

Conclusion:

Training and conditioning show dogs for success is a comprehensive process that requires time, dedication, and expertise. By implementing the right training techniques, maintaining a proper diet, and practicing regular grooming, you can enhance your show dog's performance and appearance in the show ring. Remember, responsible breeding and ethical practices are equally important in the world of show dog breeding. By adhering to these principles, you not only contribute to the betterment of the breed but also ensure the overall well-being of your show dogs.

Chapter 8: Working Dog Breeding (Police, Search and Rescue, etc.)

The Importance of Working Dogs in Various Fields

Introduction:

Working dogs have played a crucial role in various fields throughout history. From assisting farmers to protecting our communities, these dogs have proven to be invaluable companions. In this subchapter, we will explore the significance of working dogs in different areas and understand their contributions to society.

Assisting Farmers:

In the world of agriculture, working dogs have been indispensable for centuries. Whether it's herding sheep or guarding livestock, these dogs possess an innate ability to understand and respond to the needs of farmers. Their intelligence, agility, and loyalty make them perfect companions for those tending to their land.

Protecting Our Communities:

Working dogs also play a vital role in maintaining law and order in our communities. Police dogs are trained to detect drugs, explosives, and track down criminals. Their exceptional scent and hearing abilities make them an invaluable asset to law enforcement agencies. Similarly, search and rescue dogs help locate missing persons during natural disasters or accidents, saving countless lives.

Service Dogs for Special Needs Individuals:

Service dogs have become increasingly important in providing assistance to individuals with physical or mental disabilities. These highly trained dogs help their owners with everyday tasks, such as opening doors, retrieving objects, and even alerting them to potential dangers. Moreover, therapy dogs offer emotional support and comfort to people in hospitals, nursing homes, and rehabilitation centers.

Ethical Practices in Dog Breeding:

Responsible breeding practices are crucial to maintain the health and well-being of working dogs. Breeders should focus on ensuring the genetic diversity of these dogs to minimize the risk of inherited diseases. Additionally, promoting ethical breeding practices involves prioritizing the overall welfare of the dogs and ensuring they are placed in suitable environments.

Conclusion:

Working dogs have proven their worth in various fields, showcasing their exceptional skills and unwavering loyalty. Whether it's assisting farmers, protecting our communities, or providing support to individuals with special needs, their contributions are immeasurable. As dog owners and breeders, it is our responsibility to appreciate and respect the importance of these remarkable animals. By promoting responsible breeding practices, we can ensure the continued success and well-being of working dogs for generations to come.

Breeding Considerations for Working Dogs

When it comes to breeding working dogs, there are several important considerations that breeders must keep in mind in order to ensure the health, temperament, and working abilities of these special canines. Whether you are breeding police dogs, search and rescue dogs, or service dogs, the following factors should be taken into account.

First and foremost, it is crucial to select breeding pairs that possess the desired working traits and characteristics. This means carefully evaluating the lineage and pedigree of both the male and female dogs to ensure they come from a line of successful working dogs. Look for dogs with proven working abilities, excellent health records, and sound temperaments.

It is also important to consider the size and structure of the dogs. For example, if you are breeding police or search and rescue dogs, larger breeds such as German Shepherds or Belgian Malinois are often preferred due to their strength and agility. On the other hand, if you are breeding service dogs for individuals with special needs, smaller breeds like Labrador Retrievers or Golden Retrievers may be more suitable.

Additionally, breeding for desired temperament is crucial for working dogs. These dogs need to be highly trainable, focused, and confident. They should possess a strong drive to work and a natural instinct for the tasks they are trained to perform. Dogs with nervous or overly aggressive temperaments should not be used for breeding, as these traits can hinder their ability to perform their duties effectively.

Health is another vital aspect to consider in working dog breeding. Ensuring that both the male and female dogs are free from genetic diseases and health issues will help produce healthy offspring that can excel in their working roles. Regular health screenings and genetic testing should be conducted to identify any potential health risks.

Finally, responsible breeding practices should always be followed. Breeders should have a thorough understanding of genetics and breed standards, and should never breed dogs solely for profit. Ethical considerations should always be at the forefront, ensuring the well-being and welfare of the dogs involved.

In conclusion, breeding working dogs requires careful consideration of various factors, including lineage, size, temperament, health, and responsible breeding practices. By selecting breeding pairs with the desired working traits, ensuring their health and temperament, and following ethical breeding practices, breeders can contribute to the production of highly capable and successful working dogs.

Training and Preparing Working Dogs for their Roles

Working dogs play a vital role in various fields, from assisting individuals with special needs to aiding in law enforcement and search and rescue missions. To ensure these dogs are well-prepared for their roles, proper training and preparation are essential. This subchapter will delve into the key aspects of training and preparing working dogs, benefiting dog owners across various niches, including small breed dog breeding, large breed dog breeding, designer dog breeding, purebred dog breeding, rare breed dog breeding, show dog breeding, working dog breeding, service dog breeding, breeding and selling puppies for special needs individuals, and responsible breeding and ethical practices in dog breeding.

Training working dogs begins at an early age, with socialization being a crucial component. Exposing the puppies to a wide range of people, places, and situations helps them develop confidence and adaptability. Additionally, introducing them to different surfaces, sounds, and objects helps desensitize them and prepares them for their future working environments.

Obedience training is another vital aspect of preparing working dogs. Teaching them basic commands such as sit, stay, and recall lays the foundation for further specialized training. Positive reinforcement techniques, such as treats and praise, are highly effective in motivating these dogs to learn and perform desired behaviors.

Once the basics are established, working dogs can undergo specialized training tailored to their intended roles. For example, police and military dogs are trained in areas such as scent detection, apprehension, and obedience under high-stress situations. Search and rescue dogs, on the other hand, are trained to track scents, find missing persons, and navigate challenging terrain.

Service dogs require specialized training to assist individuals with disabilities. They are taught to perform tasks such as guiding the visually impaired, alerting the hearing impaired to sounds, or providing support to individuals with mobility challenges. These dogs must also exhibit impeccable manners and remain calm in various public settings.

Ethical breeding practices play a crucial role in producing working dogs with the necessary qualities for their roles. Responsible breeders carefully select parent dogs based on their temperament, health, and working traits. Genetic testing is often conducted to ensure the offspring are free from inherited disorders that could hinder their abilities.

In conclusion, training and preparing working dogs is a multifaceted process that requires early socialization, obedience training, and specialized instruction tailored to their intended roles. Whether breeding small or large breeds, purebred or designer dogs, responsible breeders play a vital role in producing working dogs with the necessary qualities. By dedicating time and resources to their development, dog owners can ensure that these working dogs excel in their roles and make a positive impact in their respective fields.

Chapter 9: Service Dog Breeding (Therapy, Assistance, etc.)

The Role and Impact of Service Dogs

Service dogs play a crucial role in the lives of many individuals, providing support, assistance, and companionship to those in need. In this subchapter, we will explore the invaluable contribution that service dogs make to society and the various ways they impact the lives of their owners.

For individuals with disabilities or special needs, service dogs offer a lifeline of independence. These highly trained canines assist their owners with daily tasks, such as opening doors, retrieving objects, or even calling for help in emergencies. They are specifically bred and trained to perform tasks that mitigate their owner's disabilities, ultimately improving their quality of life.

Service dogs are not just limited to physical disabilities, but also play a significant role in supporting individuals with mental health conditions. They can help alleviate symptoms of anxiety, depression, and post-traumatic stress disorder by providing comfort, emotional support, and a sense of security.

The impact of service dogs extends beyond the individual owner. They also contribute to the larger community by increasing public awareness and understanding of disabilities. By accompanying their owners in public spaces, service dogs help educate others about the rights and needs of individuals with disabilities, promoting inclusivity and acceptance.

In the realm of breeding, service dog breeding is a specialized niche that requires careful selection and training. Breeders who focus on producing service dogs prioritize traits such as intelligence, temperament, and trainability. They aim to create dogs that not only possess the physical abilities necessary for service work but also exhibit calmness, reliability, and a strong bond with their handlers.

Ethical breeding practices are paramount in the service dog community. Breeders must ensure the health and well-being of their dogs, conducting thorough health screenings and genetic testing to prevent passing on hereditary diseases. Responsible breeders also prioritize early socialization and provide a nurturing environment for puppies to develop into confident and well-adjusted service dogs.

The impact of service dogs on their owners is immeasurable. They provide not only physical assistance but also emotional support, companionship, and a newfound sense of freedom. By breeding and training service dogs, breeders contribute to enhancing the lives of individuals with disabilities and promoting a more inclusive society.

Whether it is a small breed, large breed, designer breed, or purebred, service dogs come in all shapes and sizes, proving that it is not just the physical attributes that matter but also the innate qualities that make them exceptional partners. The bond between a service dog and their owner is truly profound, illustrating the transformative power of these amazing animals.

Breeding Considerations for Service Dogs

Service dogs play a crucial role in providing assistance and support to individuals with disabilities or special needs. These remarkable canines are trained to perform a variety of tasks, such as guiding the visually impaired, alerting hearing-impaired individuals to sounds, or providing emotional support to those with mental health conditions. In this subchapter, we will delve into the essential considerations that dog owners, specifically those interested in breeding service dogs, should keep in mind.

When it comes to breeding service dogs, several factors must be taken into account. Firstly, health and temperament are of utmost importance. Service dogs are expected to work in challenging environments, and their overall well-being directly impacts their ability to perform their tasks effectively. Therefore, breeders should prioritize selecting parent dogs with excellent physical health, free from genetic disorders or hereditary conditions. Regular health screenings, such as hip and elbow evaluations, genetic testing, and eye exams, are essential to ensure the highest chances of producing healthy offspring.

Equally important is the temperament of the parent dogs. Service dogs must possess a calm and confident disposition, as they will encounter various situations and interact with diverse individuals. Temperament testing, including assessments for trainability, sociability, and adaptability, should be conducted to evaluate the potential breeding dogs' suitability for producing service dog candidates.

Additionally, breeders should consider the specific needs and requirements of the individuals who will receive the service dogs. Different disabilities or conditions may necessitate distinct traits in the service dogs. For example, a visually impaired person may benefit from a breed known for its exceptional sense of smell and ability to navigate obstacles efficiently. On the other hand, a person with autism may require a dog with a gentle nature and a high tolerance for repetitive behaviors. Understanding these unique needs will help breeders select the most suitable breeding pairs and increase the chances of producing successful service dog candidates.

Lastly, responsible breeding practices should always be followed. Breeders should prioritize the overall well-being and welfare of the dogs, ensuring they are provided with appropriate healthcare, nutrition, and socialization. Ethical considerations, such as avoiding overbreeding and providing lifelong support to the puppies and their new owners, are crucial in the service dog breeding community.

In conclusion, breeding service dogs requires careful consideration of health, temperament, and the specific needs of the recipients. By prioritizing these factors, breeders can contribute to the creation of highly capable and reliable service dogs that enhance the lives of individuals with disabilities or special needs.

Training and Preparing Service Dogs for their Roles

Service dogs play a crucial role in assisting individuals with disabilities or special needs, providing them with the support and companionship they need to navigate their daily lives. Whether it's guiding the blind, alerting to seizures, or providing emotional support, these dogs are trained to perform specific tasks that cater to the unique needs of their handlers. In this subchapter, we will explore the essential aspects of training and preparing service dogs for their important roles.

The first step in training a service dog is selecting the right candidate. While any breed can potentially become a service dog, certain characteristics such as intelligence, trainability, and a calm temperament are highly desirable. Various niches, including small breed dog breeding, large breed dog breeding, and designer dog breeding, can provide suitable candidates for service dog training.

Once a suitable candidate is identified, a rigorous training program should be implemented. This program should encompass obedience training, task-specific training, and socialization. Obedience training ensures that the dog is well-mannered and responsive to commands, while task-specific training focuses on teaching the dog the specific tasks they will need to perform to assist their handler. Socialization is also crucial, as service dogs need to be comfortable in various environments and around different people and animals.

Service dog breeding is a highly specialized niche that requires an understanding of the specific needs and requirements of individuals with disabilities. Responsible breeding practices ensure that the puppies are healthy, well-tempered, and have the potential to excel in their service dog roles. Breeding and selling puppies for special needs individuals require careful consideration of the genetic traits and health histories of the parents, as well as the desired traits for service dog work.

Ethical practices in dog breeding are of paramount importance. Breeders should prioritize the health and well-being of the dogs, avoiding any practices that could compromise their welfare. This includes responsible breeding, regular health screenings, and providing a nurturing and stimulating environment for the puppies.

In conclusion, training and preparing service dogs for their roles require a comprehensive understanding of the specific needs of individuals with disabilities. Dog owners involved in breeding, whether it be small breed, large breed, designer breed, or purebred, should consider the unique qualities required in service dogs. By implementing a tailored training program and adhering to responsible breeding and ethical practices, breeders can contribute to the well-being and independence of individuals with disabilities, providing them with invaluable companionship and support.

Chapter 10: Breeding and Selling Puppies for Special Needs Individuals

Understanding the Special Needs of Individuals

As dog owners, it is crucial to understand the special needs of individuals, particularly those with diverse requirements. This subchapter aims to shed light on the various considerations and responsibilities associated with breeding dogs for specific purposes and individuals with unique needs.

Small breed dog breeding necessitates an understanding of the physical limitations and vulnerabilities that these dogs may face. Their petite size requires extra care and attention to prevent injuries and accidents. Additionally, their high energy levels may require more exercise and mental stimulation to keep them happy and healthy.

On the other hand, breeding large breed dogs comes with its own set of challenges. These magnificent canines require ample space, proper training, and socialization to ensure their well-being. Understanding the potential health issues and providing appropriate care is vital for their longevity and quality of life.

Designer dog breeding, a popular trend in recent years, requires breeders to consider the unique characteristics and needs of each crossbreed. By understanding the traits of the parent breeds, breeders can produce dogs that possess desired qualities while minimizing potential health risks associated with certain purebred lines.

Purebred dog breeding emphasizes the preservation and improvement of specific breed standards. Breeders must be knowledgeable about the breed's history, temperament, and health concerns to produce healthy and well-structured puppies that conform to breed standards.

In the realm of rare breed dog breeding, breeders play a crucial role in preserving and promoting these unique and often endangered breeds. Understanding their specific needs, genetic predispositions, and potential health issues is essential to ensure their continued existence.

For those involved in show dog breeding, a deep understanding of breed standards, grooming techniques, and training methods is necessary. Breeders must strive to produce dogs that exemplify the breed's characteristics and possess the temperament required to succeed in the show ring.

Working dog breeding, including police and search and rescue dogs, demands breeders to select dogs with exceptional intelligence, stamina, and drive. Understanding the specific requirements of these roles is crucial to produce highly skilled and reliable working dogs.

Service dog breeding, aimed at providing therapy and assistance to individuals with disabilities, requires breeders to focus on temperament, trainability, and health. These dogs must possess a calm and patient nature to effectively aid those in need.

Breeding and selling puppies for special needs individuals requires breeders to understand the specific requirements of these individuals, whether it be for therapy, medical assistance, or emotional support. Matching the right dog with the right person is paramount for a successful partnership.

Finally, responsible breeding and ethical practices in dog breeding underpin all the aforementioned niches. Breeders must prioritize the health and well-being of their dogs, ensuring proper veterinary care, genetic testing, and responsible breeding practices are adhered to.

In conclusion, understanding the special needs of individuals is crucial for dog owners and breeders alike. By recognizing the unique requirements of different niches such as small breed, large breed, designer, purebred, rare breed, show, working, service, and special needs dog breeding, we can ensure the well-being and happiness of both dogs and their owners. Responsible breeding practices and ethical considerations form the foundation of a thriving and compassionate dog breeding community.

Breeding Considerations for Puppies for Special Needs

Bringing a new puppy into your home is an exciting and joyful experience, but when you are considering breeding puppies for special needs individuals, there are additional factors to take into account. Ensuring that these puppies are well-suited to their future owners' unique needs requires careful planning and consideration. In this subchapter, we will explore the breeding considerations for puppies destined to become special needs companions.

One of the most crucial aspects to consider is the temperament and behavior of the parent dogs. For puppies to succeed as special needs companions, they must possess qualities such as patience, calmness, and a willingness to learn. Selecting parent dogs with these traits is essential to ensure that the puppies inherit the right temperament and disposition.

Health is another vital consideration when breeding puppies for special needs. It is essential to choose parents that are free from genetic disorders and have undergone thorough health screenings. Special needs individuals often require dogs that are physically healthy and resilient, as they may rely heavily on their canine companions for support and assistance.

When it comes to purebred dog breeding, it is crucial to carefully select breeds that are known for their suitability as special needs companions. Breeds such as Labradors, Golden Retrievers, and Poodles have proven to be excellent choices due to their intelligence, trainability, and gentle nature. However, it is important to note that designer dog breeding can also yield successful results, as long as the chosen breeds possess the necessary traits.

Responsible breeding practices are paramount when it comes to breeding puppies for special needs individuals. It is crucial to ensure that both parent dogs are well-cared for, receive regular veterinary check-ups, and are adequately socialized. Additionally, ethical considerations should be taken into account, such as avoiding excessive breeding and ensuring that all puppies find suitable and loving homes.

Lastly, it is important to recognize that each special needs individual may have unique requirements. Some may need dogs with specific training, while others may require hypoallergenic breeds. As a breeder, understanding the specific needs of the individuals you are serving is crucial to matching them with the most suitable puppy.

Breeding puppies for special needs individuals is a noble endeavor that requires careful thought and consideration. By selecting parent dogs with the right temperament, prioritizing health, and practicing responsible breeding, you can contribute to the creation of exceptional canine companions that will bring joy and assistance to those in need.

Matching and Placing Puppies with Special Needs Individuals

Introduction:

Finding the perfect companion can be a challenge, especially for individuals with special needs. This subchapter explores the important task of matching and placing puppies with special needs individuals. Whether it's for therapy, assistance, or simply companionship, this process requires careful consideration and ethical practices. As responsible dog owners and breeders, it is our duty to ensure the best possible match for both the puppy and the special needs individual.

Understanding Special Needs:

Before embarking on the journey of matching and placing puppies, it is crucial to have a deep understanding of the specific needs of individuals with disabilities. Whether it's physical, mental, or emotional, each special needs individual requires a unique set of qualities in their future companion. It is important to consider factors such as size, temperament, energy level, and specific training needs when selecting a puppy for a special needs individual.

Screening and Evaluation:

The first step in matching puppies with special needs individuals is a thorough screening and evaluation process. This involves assessing the individual's requirements and preferences, as well as evaluating the puppy's temperament, health, and potential for training. It is essential to involve professionals such as therapists, trainers, and veterinarians to ensure an accurate assessment.

Training and Socialization:

Once the perfect match has been made, it is important to focus on training and socialization. Special needs individuals may require specific training techniques or assistance with tasks such as therapy or mobility support. Ensuring that the puppy is well-socialized and exposed to various environments is also vital for their successful integration into the special needs individual's life.

Ongoing Support and Care:

Matching and placing puppies with special needs individuals is not a one-time event. It requires ongoing support and care from the breeder, the special needs individual, and their families. Regular check-ins, access to resources, and guidance on training and healthcare are essential for the well-being of both the puppy and the special needs individual.

Conclusion:

Matching and placing puppies with special needs individuals is a rewarding and life-changing process. As dog owners, breeders, and enthusiasts, we have the power to make a positive impact on the lives of individuals with disabilities. By understanding their specific needs, conducting careful screenings, providing appropriate training, and offering ongoing support, we can ensure a successful and fulfilling partnership between a special needs individual and their furry companion. Let us embrace responsible breeding and ethical practices to create these life-changing connections.

Chapter 11: Responsible Breeding and Ethical Practices in Dog Breeding

The Importance of Responsible Breeding

In the fascinating world of dog breeding, it is crucial to understand the importance of responsible breeding. Whether you are involved in small breed dog breeding, large breed dog breeding, designer dog breeding, purebred dog breeding, rare breed dog breeding, show dog breeding, working dog breeding, service dog breeding, or breeding and selling puppies for special needs individuals, responsible breeding practices are the foundation for the well-being of both the dogs and their future owners.

Responsible breeding goes beyond simply producing cute and desirable puppies. It involves a commitment to the health, temperament, and overall quality of the breed. By practicing responsible breeding, you contribute to the preservation and improvement of the canine gene pool.

One of the key aspects of responsible breeding is prioritizing the health of the dogs. This means carefully selecting breeding pairs that are free from genetic diseases and hereditary conditions. By conducting thorough health screenings and genetic testing, breeders can significantly reduce the risk of passing on these issues to future generations. Responsible breeders also prioritize the overall well-being of the dogs, ensuring they receive proper nutrition, exercise, and veterinary care.

Temperament is another crucial factor in responsible breeding. Dogs with stable and predictable temperaments are more likely to become well-adjusted family pets or successful working dogs. Responsible breeders carefully evaluate the temperament of their breeding dogs and select pairs that complement each other's personalities, aiming to produce offspring with desirable temperamental traits.

Ethical practices are at the core of responsible breeding. This includes providing a safe and clean environment for the dogs, socializing and training them from an early age, and maintaining open communication with puppy buyers. Responsible breeders also prioritize finding suitable homes for their puppies, ensuring they go to responsible owners who are prepared to provide lifelong care and commitment.

By promoting responsible breeding, we can combat the issues associated with irresponsible breeding practices, such as overbreeding, inbreeding, and the production of unhealthy or poorly socialized puppies. Responsible breeders play a vital role in maintaining the integrity and reputation of the dog breeding community.

Whether you are a breeder or a dog owner, it is essential to support and promote responsible breeding practices. By doing so, we can ensure that future generations of dogs are healthy, well-adjusted, and bring joy and companionship to their owners. Together, let's strive for excellence in the art of crossbreeding canines while upholding the values of responsibility, ethics, and the well-being of our beloved four-legged companions.

Ethical Considerations in Dog Breeding

Introduction:

Dog breeding is a complex and multifaceted process that requires careful thought and consideration. As dog owners and breeders, it is our responsibility to ensure the health, well-being, and ethical treatment of our beloved companions. This subchapter will delve into the various ethical considerations that need to be taken into account when engaging in dog breeding, regardless of the specific niche or purpose.

1. Health and Genetic Considerations:

One of the primary ethical concerns in dog breeding is the health and genetic well-being of the dogs involved. Breeders must prioritize the health screening of their breeding dogs, including genetic testing for known hereditary conditions. This ensures that puppies are not born with debilitating health issues and promotes the overall health of the breed.

2. Responsible Breeding Practices:

Responsible breeders carefully select their breeding pairs based on temperament, health, and conformation to breed standards. They strive to improve the breed while avoiding excessive inbreeding and genetic bottlenecks. Breeding should not be undertaken solely for financial gain, but with the intention of promoting healthy, well-rounded dogs.

3. Overpopulation and Rescue Considerations:

Ethical breeders are mindful of the overpopulation crisis in shelters and take steps to reduce the number of unwanted dogs. They advocate for responsible pet ownership, promote spaying and neutering, and actively support rescue organizations. By taking these measures, breeders contribute to the well-being of all dogs, not just their own.

4. Transparency and Education:

Ethical breeders are transparent about their breeding practices, health testing, and the conditions in which their dogs are raised. They actively educate potential puppy buyers about the breed's characteristics, needs, and potential health issues. This allows buyers to make informed decisions and ensures that the puppies find suitable homes.

5. Lifetime Responsibility:

Ethical breeders recognize that their responsibility extends beyond the moment of sale. They provide ongoing support and guidance to puppy buyers throughout the dog's lifetime. They willingly take back dogs they have bred if the owner can no longer care for them, ensuring that no dog ends up in a shelter or unsuitable environment.

Conclusion:

Ethical considerations in dog breeding are of utmost importance in ensuring the well-being of dogs and the preservation of breeds. By adhering to responsible breeding practices, prioritizing health and genetics, and actively working to reduce overpopulation, breeders contribute positively to the world of dogs. It is through ethical practices that we can preserve the beauty and diversity of our beloved canine companions for generations to come.

Breeding Standards and Codes of Ethics

Breeding dogs is a complex and rewarding endeavor that requires careful planning, knowledge, and a commitment to ethical practices. In this subchapter, we will explore the importance of breeding standards and codes of ethics in various niches of dog breeding, including small breed, large breed, designer dog, purebred, rare breed, show dog, working dog, service dog, breeding for special needs individuals, and responsible breeding.

Breeding standards serve as guidelines to ensure that breeders are producing healthy, well-tempered, and genetically sound dogs. These standards outline the desired traits and characteristics of each breed, promoting consistency and maintaining breed integrity. By adhering to these standards, breeders can preserve and improve the quality of their breeds, as well as protect the welfare of the dogs they breed.

Codes of ethics play a crucial role in promoting responsible and ethical breeding practices. They set forth a set of principles and guidelines that breeders must follow to ensure the well-being of their dogs and the integrity of the breeding process. These codes often include provisions on proper socialization, health testing, genetic screening, responsible breeding age, and responsible ownership.

In small breed dog breeding, breeders should focus on producing dogs that are well-suited for apartment living, have good temperaments, and are free from common health issues associated with their breeds. Large breed dog breeders, on the other hand, should prioritize the prevention of genetic disorders associated with their breeds, such as hip dysplasia or bloat.

Designer dog breeders should carefully select the parent breeds to create healthy and desirable crossbreeds, avoiding the pitfalls of inbreeding or poor selection. Purebred dog breeders should work towards preserving the breed's heritage, maintaining breed standards, and minimizing the risks of genetic disorders that may be prevalent within specific breeds.

Rare breed dog breeders play a vital role in preserving and protecting endangered breeds, ensuring their survival for future generations. Show dog breeders should aim to produce dogs that not only meet breed standards but also possess the necessary qualities to excel in the show ring.

Working dog breeders, including those breeding police or search and rescue dogs, should focus on producing dogs with the appropriate drives, temperament, and physical abilities required for their specific roles. Similarly, service dog breeders should prioritize breeding dogs with the right temperament, intelligence, and trainability to serve as therapy or assistance dogs.

For breeders specializing in breeding and selling puppies for special needs individuals, it is crucial to select dogs with the appropriate temperament and trainability to meet the specific needs of their recipients. Responsible breeding practices, such as proper socialization, early neurological stimulation, and health testing, are essential in ensuring the success of these partnerships.

Overall, breeding standards and codes of ethics are critical in promoting responsible and ethical practices in dog breeding. By following these guidelines, breeders can contribute to the betterment of their chosen breeds, enhance the lives of their dogs, and ensure the satisfaction of new dog owners.

Chapter 12: Conclusion

The Future of Designer Dog Breeding

In recent years, designer dog breeding has gained immense popularity among dog owners and enthusiasts alike. These crossbreeds, born out of the combination of two purebred dogs, have captured the hearts of many with their unique looks, temperaments, and health benefits. As we delve into the future of designer dog breeding, it is crucial to understand its significance within various niches of dog breeding.

For small breed dog breeding enthusiasts, designer dogs offer a fresh perspective on creating adorable companions that are perfectly suited for apartment living. Breeds like the Maltipoo (Maltese and Poodle mix) or the Cavachon (Cavalier King Charles Spaniel and Bichon Frise mix) are ideal for those seeking a compact and low-shedding companion.

On the other end of the spectrum, large breed dog breeding enthusiasts can explore the possibilities of creating majestic and gentle giants through designer dog breeding. The Bernedoodle (Bernese Mountain Dog and Poodle mix) or the Goldendoodle (Golden Retriever and Poodle mix) are examples of such magnificent breeds that combine the best qualities of their parent breeds.

For those interested in rare or unique breeds, designer dog breeding opens up a whole new world of possibilities. By carefully selecting and crossing two rare or lesser-known breeds, breeders can create extraordinary and exclusive companions that are sure to turn heads at dog shows or in the neighborhood park.

Designer dog breeding also plays a crucial role in the field of service dog breeding. By selectively crossing specific breeds known for their intelligence, temperament, and trainability, breeders can produce exceptional service dogs that excel in therapy, assistance, and search and rescue work.

However, as designer dog breeding continues to evolve, responsible breeding practices must be at the forefront. Breeders must prioritize the health and well-being of the dogs, ensuring proper genetic testing, and avoiding excessive inbreeding. Ethical practices are essential to ensure the long-term viability and welfare of these new crossbreeds.

In conclusion, the future of designer dog breeding holds great promise for dog owners and enthusiasts across various niches. Whether you are a fan of small breeds, large breeds, rare breeds, or working and service dogs, designer dog breeding can offer a new dimension of companionship, functionality, and beauty. As long as responsible breeding practices and ethical considerations are embraced, the world of designer dog breeding will continue to flourish, providing us with incredible canine companions for years to come.

The Impact of Responsible and Ethical Breeding Practices

As dog owners and enthusiasts, we have a responsibility to ensure that our beloved companions are bred and raised in a safe and ethical manner. The impact of responsible and ethical breeding practices is not only crucial for the health and well-being of individual dogs, but it also has far-reaching effects on the entire canine population.

In the realm of small breed dog breeding, responsible practices ensure that the health and temperament of these delicate creatures are prioritized. By selecting breeding pairs based on health screenings and genetic testing, breeders can minimize the risk of passing on hereditary diseases and disorders. Ethical breeders also focus on providing proper socialization and early life experiences to ensure that small breed dogs grow up to be well-adjusted and confident.

On the other end of the spectrum, large breed dog breeding requires careful attention to prevent common health issues such as hip dysplasia and heart conditions. Responsible breeders work closely with veterinarians and utilize genetic testing to identify potential health risks. By selecting breeding pairs with sound health and temperament, they contribute to the overall improvement of large breed dogs and help reduce the prevalence of genetic disorders.

For those involved in designer dog breeding, responsible practices are crucial to avoid the pitfalls of creating unhealthy or unstable crossbreeds. Responsible breeders carefully consider the genetics of both parent breeds, ensuring that the resulting crossbreed inherits the best traits from each side while minimizing health risks. This dedication to responsible breeding helps maintain the integrity and popularity of designer dogs.

Purebred dog breeding also benefits greatly from responsible and ethical practices. Breeders who prioritize health screenings and genetic testing contribute to the overall well-being of purebred dogs. Additionally, responsible breeders work to preserve and improve breed standards, ensuring the long-term viability and integrity of purebred dog breeds.

Responsible and ethical breeding practices are also essential in rare breed dog breeding. By carefully controlling breeding programs, breeders can help prevent the extinction of rare breeds and promote genetic diversity. This, in turn, ensures the long-term survival and continuation of these unique and often historically significant breeds.

Whether it's show dog breeding, working dog breeding, or service dog breeding, responsible and ethical practices are the foundation for success. Show dogs must not only possess physical beauty but also sound health and temperament. Working and service dogs require exceptional traits such as intelligence, trainability, and stability. By prioritizing these qualities and breeding with care, responsible breeders contribute to the success and reliability of these specialized dogs.

Lastly, responsible breeding plays a vital role in providing puppies for special needs individuals. By carefully selecting breeding pairs with the right temperament and characteristics, breeders can produce puppies that are suitable for individuals with specific needs. This enhances the quality of life for both the individuals and their furry companions.

In conclusion, the impact of responsible and ethical breeding practices cannot be overstated. From small breed dogs to large breeds, designer dogs to purebreds, rare breeds to show dogs, and working dogs to service dogs, responsible breeding practices are essential. By prioritizing health, temperament, and genetic diversity, responsible breeders contribute to the betterment of the entire canine population and ensure that our beloved companions thrive for generations to come.

Final Thoughts and Recommendations for Dog Owners

As we come to the end of this book, it is important to reflect on the knowledge and insights gained about the art of crossbreeding canines. Whether you are a small breed dog breeder, large breed dog breeder, designer dog breeder, purebred dog breeder, rare breed dog breeder, or even a show dog breeder, the principles discussed throughout this book are applicable to all dog owners and breeders. In this final subchapter, we will provide some valuable recommendations and thoughts for dog owners across various niches.

First and foremost, responsible breeding and ethical practices should be at the forefront of every dog owner's mind. Breeding should always be done with the intention of improving the overall health, temperament, and well-being of the breed. It is crucial to prioritize health testing, genetic screening, and proper care for both the dam and sire to ensure the production of healthy puppies.

For those involved in breeding and selling puppies for special needs individuals, it is essential to understand the specific requirements and temperaments required for service dogs or therapy animals. Proper socialization and training are crucial to ensure that these dogs can fulfill their duties effectively and provide the necessary support to their owners.

Furthermore, regardless of the niche, all dog owners should prioritize the overall welfare of their canines. This includes providing a suitable living environment, a balanced diet, regular exercise, and proper veterinary care. Dogs thrive when they are given love, attention, and mental stimulation, so it is essential to invest time in their well-being.

Another recommendation for dog owners is to consider adopting from shelters or rescue organizations. Many wonderful dogs are in need of loving homes, and by adopting, you are saving a life and giving a deserving dog a second chance. Mixed breed dogs can be just as loving and loyal as purebred dogs, and they often come with fewer health issues.

Lastly, as a dog owner, it is important to continue educating yourself about canine health, behavior, and training. Attend seminars, workshops, or join online communities where you can exchange knowledge and experiences with fellow dog owners and breeders. By staying informed, you can provide the best care for your furry companions and contribute to the betterment of the canine community.

In conclusion, being a dog owner is a privilege and responsibility. By following ethical breeding practices, prioritizing the welfare of your dogs, considering adoption, and continuously learning, you can provide a loving and fulfilling life for your canine companions. Let us all work together to ensure the well-being and happiness of dogs across all breeds and niches.

www.ingramcontent.com/pod-product-compliance
Lightning Source LLC
Chambersburg PA
CBHW051807130726

47987CB00003B/1153